The House with the Mansard Roof

The House
with the
Mansard
Roof

Matthew Brennan

The Backwaters Press

Also by Matthew Brennan

Poetry
Seeing in the Dark, Hawkhead Press (1993)
The Music of Exile, Cloverdale Books (1994)
The Sea-Crossing of Saint Brendan, Birch Book Press (2008)

Critical Studies
Wordsworth, Turner, and Romantic Landscape, Camden House (1987)
The Gothic Psyche, Camden House (1997)

First Printing: July 2009

Published by: The Backwaters Press
                  Greg Kosmicki, Rich Wyatt, Editors
                  3502 N. 52nd Street
                  Omaha, Nebraska 68104-3506

                  thebackwaterspress@gmail.com
                  http://www.thebackwaterspress.com

                  ISBN: 978-1-935218-10-4

Acknowledgments

Thanks to the editors of the following publications for first printing these poems, some of which have been revised:

Blue Unicorn: "Before Taking Your Picture I Think Of," "Watching the Sun Set from the Mount St. Francis Cemetery," "Winter Landscape," "Regarding the Old Poets"
California Quarterly: "Granary Days"
Concho River Review: "After Delivering My Son to the Ex"
Descant: "Signs of Life," "Weekend Retreat in Brown County"
Firefly Magazine: "Summer Storm"
Green Hills Literary Lantern: "Waiting for Green," "Memorial Field, 1973"
Heartland Review: "Highway 40, Stilesville"
Iambs & Trochees: "The Fair Oaks Apartments Revisited"
Lake Effect: "December Sunset in Terre Haute"
Light Quarterly: "Adagio for Middle Age While Sitting Outside in Late October"
The MacGuffin: "Lake Petworth, Sunrise"
Merton Seasonal: "The Sublime"
Mid-America Poetry Review: "At Mercouri's Restaurant"
Mildred: "Skylights"
National Catholic Reporter: "Father Louis' Nose Job"
Notre Dame Review: "Fall Plowing"
Number One: "Thomas Hart Benton Rebuts the Museum Director Who Dismissed His New Deal Murals"
Passages North: "Nights Our House Comes to Life"
Paterson Literary Review: "Illuminations," "A Divorcée's Revenge," "Summer of '36"
Pivot: "Merton in Love"; "Henry James at 57"
Poem: "Farm Houses"; "Turning Point in the European Theater," "Drought," "Preheating"
Poet Lore: "Washington Avenue Bridge," "Reprise"
Sewanee Review: "After the Sack of South Carolina"
South Dakota Review: "The Gargoyle in Our Backyard," "Prohibition," "Eads Bridge, St. Louis, 1935," "The House with the Mansard Roof"
Sycamore Review: "Leaving San Francisco Early," "Clairvoyance"
Terre Haute Living: "September 22, in Indiana"

Westview: "On the Beara Peninsula," "Night-Piece in Cork at the
        Ambassador Hotel," "The Past," "First Kiss"
Yalobusha Review: "Epiphanies"

"Downtown at Dusk" was part of the 2006-2007 Shared Spaces/Shared
Voices program of the Arts Council of Indianapolis that placed poems
on Indianapolis buses and printed them in a catalog. "Farm Houses,"
"Fall Plowing," "Eads Bridge," "Prohibition," "Summer of '36" (as
"Unemployment"), "Thomas Hart Benton," "Highway 40" (as "Rural
Route, in November"), and "Drought" appeared in the limited-edition
chapbook *American Scenes: Poems on WPA Artworks* (2001); "Preheating"
and "Nights Our House Comes to Life" appeared in *The Music of Exile*
(1994); and "A Divorcée's Revenge" and "Skylights" appeared in *Seeing in
the Dark* (1993).

This book was written with the assistance of a summer grant from the Indiana
State U. Arts Endowment Committee. Special thanks to Rod Torreson, Robert
McPhillips, David Vancil, John Christie, Mick Kennedy, and Dave Malone.

The House with the Mansard Roof

I.

II.

III. desire, love - not as strong as first two sections

sometime don't rise about personal

rest of bunch

IV.

desire / love w/ religious overtone

V.

poetry / writers / salvation agony + death

In memory of my grandparents
William A. Brennan and Jane Cannon Brennan
Louise Cramer Simon and Jerome I. Simon, M.D.

I

Waiting for Green

For my father and my son

I was a kid who hated his dad's guts: shin-deep
in our front lawn, shouldering a push-mower
through a growth shrub-thick, I knew inside
his lung a tumor grapefruit-sized was sprouting
quicker than crabgrass, swifter than
fire in straw. I'd wished it would not rain
on us again and Dad was dead already,
his grave's weeds long as bamboo and still growing,
like hair in a closed coffin.
       Eight years later,
the day my parents met their only grandson,
I drove our Dodge in the late August heat
to the hardware store. There, my dad would buy
us three rotating fans for our cheap basement
apartment, whose few windows squinted into
a parking lot. My son, just six-weeks-old,
napped in his stuffy room. At a red light
we watched a boy cutting a dry, brown yard:
Dad said, "I never thought I'd see this day";
the light changed, and our lives moved on for years.
Now Mother and Dad are both dead. But I've learned
the urgency Dad felt about our blood.

Ten years ago a sheriff called — I raced
against the clock and blackness blooming
in Alabama where I sped to save
my son from a second night in juvenile jail
and from spring break's stupidity. Lost, I turned wrong
onto a bumpy gravel path that took me past
some trailer homes with plastic sheets
for doors and slits for windows, dark and open
as sockets whose eyes are gone. But they saw
my fear when I turned around. My headlights

flooded through their dead-end homes, like caskets
buried amid blinding, wild woods. Soon after,
in an old red-brick building, I found him
at last, wide-eyed and wakened from his dreams
built on sand, miles and miles from Mobile's sprawl
and the green lights we passed through on our long way home.

sometimes transitions not so smooth
but good wraps, compelling

Nights Our House Comes to Life

Some nights in midwinter when the creek clogs
With ice and the spines of fir trees stiffen
Under a blank, frozen sky,
On these nights our house comes to life.
It happens when you're half asleep:
A sudden crack, a fractured dream, you bolting
Upright—but all you can hear is the clock
Your great-grandfather found in 1860
And smuggled here from Dublin for his future bride,
A being as unknown to him then as she is now
To you, a being as distant as the strangers
Who built this house, and died in this room
Some cold, still night, like tonight,
When all that was heard were the rhythmic clicks
Of a pendulum, and something, barely audible,
Moving on the dark landing of the attic stairs.

Night-Piece in Cork at the Ambassador Hotel

Unable to sleep at 3 a.m., I go
to the open window of my third-floor room,
looming high up on Military Hill:
Downtown unfolds beneath me like a quilt,
the river stitching this hillside to uplands
in the south. Farther off, beyond the darkness,
the river herringbones into the sea.
Tonight, there is no light from stars for miles.

It makes me think of my own flesh and blood,
the brood that came from Tipperary
and County Cork, but now are gone and never
known by us. They must have trooped to town
on market days, before first dawn light,
when stars were threads in the dark open skies,
furrows in fields that later led them home.

The lights that pulse in this too-quiet night
can't animate the dead and can't return
to Cork what shined in their long-ended lives.
But surely some illumination comes
from rooftops and lamps of Brennans listed still
in the Cork city phone book. Even now
I see the surface of the river glow,
a candle lit on All Souls' Day that flickers

until the wick burns out and its last light
changes to smoke, the way a river empties
into a bay, its water sewn into the sea.

nice

The Past

To make it live, as Vermeer tried
for Arnolfini, approximates
how memory works, the texture of
the way things were. But what once flared —

a spot of time, vividly fixed
in the mind's permanent collection —
always fades, like the sun's rays
reflected from a pewter plate.

Take Lake Calhoun, a photograph,
1980: it shows a mist
obscuring the sun one fall morning
in Minnesota, but the print

itself is dim, and even though
the sunrise happened, something's lost
to the outer eye — so only feeling
for the fleeting light survives.

Prohibition

In Ben Shahn's Depression mural, Feds <u>force</u>
foaming beer from sixteen-gallon kegs down
an open drain. It <u>flushes</u> through the city's sewers
and mixes with rainwatered muck that runs
into the river, whose <u>black, viscous surface</u>
suds at night like mugs of Guinness stout.

Ben Shahn leaves the rest untold: the Feds
lowering their fedoras' brims and <u>sidling</u>
from afternoon light into the dark booths
of some back-alley joint, its windows boarded,
its door unmarked like bottles they pass back
and forth. At home, my grandmother — divorced
and poor but lifelong loyalist of Hoover's ilk —
sips her last glass of bathtub gin, then makes

her first and final radical move: she'll throw
her vote to Roosevelt, and vows never again
to swill near-beer at Bevo Mill — but never
forgot those nights when, under stars, she danced
away her sober youth in the arms of men
with chests <u>like beer barrels, empty and dark.</u>

Summer of '36

After a WPA print by Jolan Gross-Bettelheim

1

In the lithograph *Employment Office*, three figures
look out from the glint of a single bulb. A man
in his mid-fifties barely grazes the light.
This man might be my grandfather, in St. Louis,
the hot summer of '36. I see him lying
awake at dawn, already sticky in the sheets,
dreading the day. Mourning doves
coo from the roof of a neighbor's flat; soon,
he'll rise and in worn leather shoes will hoof
down Chouteau Avenue to Grand, then pound
fifty blistering blocks of pavement north
where "twelve experienced men are wanted
to wire some ceilings in the city's public schools."

2

Out before eight, he spies last evening's *Post*
in O'Brien's bushes and breaks stride to glimpse
the headlines—"REDS BLAMED FOR WORKERS' RIOTS";
"BANK FAILS"; "FARMERS MARCH WITH PITCHFORKS."
He skips the weather and reads the clouds that cloak
the skies and just two blocks past Chouteau
sweep the boulevard like crows. Now gutters
and drainpipes drench the sidewalks and streets,
which westward disappear behind a gray veneer,
while rain typewrites on Grandpa's cap; it blots
the swooshing cars and office buildings,
where people work in dry starched shirts. He pushes
onward, his socks so soaked brown bubbles ooze
like oil through the eyeholes when his feet squeeze
against the slippery surface. With the view

blacked out, he scans displays in windows filing by:
the cornucopia of capitalism out of reach
behind plate glass — pin-striped suits, mannequins
in minks and pearls, Persian rugs, ice boxes.

3

He passes two men — wet coats on hangers
who beg for nickels — and shivers with
a premonition: his feet heavy as bricks
and the few jobs filled overnight
by the Ward's political machine. He stamps
ahead no matter what and dares the dam inside
to burst; he stands in line till five.
                                        Turned away
at last, though hungry and tired, and who
in hell knows how he'll make the rent,
he still can mouth his mantra: all that happens
is for the best. And then he bends to tie his laces,
aching bones and all, and finds beside a sewer
the bus pass that gets him two traffic lights from home.

Eads Bridge, St. Louis, 1935

After *The Bridges*, a WPA print by John M. Foster

Under Eads Bridge, the homeless gathered
In shadows, like *staffage* in dimly lit
Dutch paintings. Mornings, they would watch
The waves for hours, their poles propped
From rocks, their lines sunk into
The sluicing, liquid mud where stray
Catfish could be caught—if good luck struck.

One Sunday in June, Grandfather, tired
From double shifts at City Hospital, embarked
On a patron's pleasure boat to cruise up
And down the brown, indifferent waters.
By two, the sun glared, boiling the thick soup
Of bouillabaisse that circled them, and burned
The metal deck and rails like spoons left on
A hot stove. He could take it no longer:

Stripped to his boxers, wiped his brow,
Then jumped, jackknifing into
The pliant muck; immediately, cold currents
Rushed up to enfold his overheated flesh;
Eyes closed, he felt refreshed—but then uprising
To breathe in air again, he found a ring
Of turds about to hook around his neck
And instantly knew this down-and-out decade
Was not about to let him go.

Clairvoyance

For Jane C. Brennan, 1888-1973

I wake to winds crashing against
gutters and glass — the whole house

shudders, shakes me out of bottomless
sleep. Apparitional light is oozing

through slanted miniblinds and grazing
the wall beside my bed, like mist

clouding a mirror: half-asleep, I dig
up my grandmother's wish to wake

some night and find her mother back,
diaphanous in the dark, but alive.

She'd scared me when she said this,
she who, at five, was exorcised

by two priests chanting Latin and sure
she'd seen beneath the heaps on graves,

seen through the soon-to-die, their souls
like train lights tunneling into

winter darkness. Now, all things outside
are dim; the single streetlamp's out, my glasses

off, but suddenly I feel her back —
remembering that April afternoon

it snowed and that black hearse which carried her
away, its high beams on, as if to see

into a space no other car could reach.

The Sublime

The sun is god.
> — J.M.W. Turner

When Turner lay dying, his curtained bed
Butted against the shuttered glass, he saw
Light landing on the window ledge like rain —
Just out of reach. His dry, paint-splotched hand opened
To hold the golden glow. He closed his eyes.

He dreamed of barges and freighters docked;
Leftward, a row of domes, smokestacks, and spires;
Rightward, a vacant pier that juts into
A bay of haze and black waters — and all
On fire from blotches burning far beyond

Toward which the ship in the center moves and grasps
For something to tug it from the coming darkness.

II

Fall Plowing

After a WPA painting by Grant Wood, 1931

America's begun to go to bed hungry,
    but everywhere, in Iowa, the land
        looks tillable: the fields slope

and roll in forms palpable to the naked eye,
    which slides into Wood's imagined span
        like a lover's gentle hand; it first works over

a silken hip, then slowly curves inward
    to smooth some rows of folded flesh—
        until the gaze, uprising, abruptly empalms

two looming parabolic shapes, ground so
    green and round with hope it feeds you more
        the more you look.
                But these twin hills

resemble, too, a still-life's bowls, turned over
    and empty, like the flat, fruitless hands
        you hold back from the canvas.

Farm Houses

After Michael Gallegher's *Stoney Forms*, 1939

On Mangan's farm it's always winter:
Another gray day in early March
When cold branch-breaking winds lash
The hunched, scabbed backs of willow trees,
Their long black branches shaking fists

At the indifferent sky, begging pardons
From another scourge. It's hard to believe
It thawed last week—grass under trees was about
To sprout amid the garden's snow, and tulips
And daffodils could not be far behind.

But now that ground is like tundra again,
Glass rattles in barn windows, tries to break
Free from the warped hands of shashes that hold
Them in, that have endured dark nights too long
And will lose their grip next time it snows.

Highway 40, Stilesville

The sky, T-shirt gray, blackens as if wet
With sweat from long labor as the car hurries
Westward where wilderness sleeps and snow flurries

And whirls, the sawdust of evening. The night,
A dirty woodworker, has cast aside bad news—
Curled shavings, splinters, unused knots

Of rotten boards—and from deep inside the mind
Has carved a luminous shape, its light
Like the neon sign in a one-bar town,

Beyond which darkness waits, silent and bare
As a body ready to return to earth.

The House with the Mansard Roof

The house behind us waits for better days.
It's been betrayed eight times since we moved in
ten years ago, but was built long before
the road was paved. The mansard roof, which rises
high above both homes flanking it, reflects
the past; the shingles shine like silver plates
in early morning light. The western walls

wear shingles too — but in the shade, they're jagged,
nubby meth teeth. Below, the back porch sags,
weighted down by decades of deadbeats
who trash the place and then bolt, grinning through
a pick-up's greasy glass. The yard out back
becomes a mudslide when it rains; no matter who's
passed through, they've left a landfill of their lives,
furrows of beer cans, butts, and pissed-on chairs.

But now the furniture and crap are gone.
The windows — blocked with plywood boards —
keep out the light. And yet the inner rooms are rich
in darkness, like black earth beneath the sills,
where weeds with bride-white lace have taken root.

December Sunset in Terre Haute

At five, dusk passes into night, the sky
Bloodshot, a half-closed eye.
Downtown, the morning snow still lies
Along the shabby streets, the feathery white
Of dirty cuffs and collar.

No footprints in the unswept stretch
Of shops that shut by noon and bars that never
Opened. The roofs of cars are gleaming
Like labels on beer bottles. Everything's
Regressed into an alcoholic dream.

And everyone's holed up — except
The crows, who flocked to town
Like flies to rotten fruit. Their long black wings
Fan the lime-white tops of trees, the blades
Of helicopters casting darkness

Below, on a surface crystalline still
Like glasses emptied of Merlot.

Drought: A Farm Wife's Diary

After Jakob Kainen's lithograph, c. 1935

Yesterday, we drove for sixty miles —
Round trip — and passed a single car,
Its patched tent lashed on top, its tires

Weighed down by a washtub and iron stove,
Heavy with sadness. As they drove away
The sky behind them glowed like ripened wheat.

We must stay put, can't sell or rent this land
We've worked for thirty years. At night,
I lie awake, a body at the morgue,

Or dream the worst has come. Last night,
Round three, I dozed and saw the blood-brown cloud
Drive down the hill, unloading silt

In mounds that buried tree stumps, fences,
And then our kitchen floor; I woke
When dust had drifted within an inch

Of my neck. No, we won't default.
But summer rains must come, or seed
Will sprout but die, stillborn below the ground —

Our only place to stand and watch for clouds:
Like chosen people in the desert, we
Scan the flat, dry sand — as far as eyes

Can see — for signs our gods might come again.

Thomas Hart Benton Rebuts the Museum Director Who Dismissed His New Deal Murals

If it were up to me alone, there'd be no more
museums — graveyards run by fops like you
who squeeze out pennies for the art you take
that doesn't pay my boy's piano lessons —
or even a few weeks of turpentine.
And who's fool enough to tiptoe through most
museums anyway? American people go
to corner bars, juke joints and bawdy houses,
Kiwanis Clubs and barber shops — or any
old place except high-brow embalming rooms.

In '39, I lent bandleader Billy Rose
my oil *Persephone* to show three weeks
in his downtown club: more than 40,000 saw
the brunette beauty queen, sprawled out beneath
a tree like Garbo in the nude — can you
imagine that? — and yet not even one
art critic dared to see the churl curled round
the bark as a mirror of his second self.

Father Louis' Nose Job

A monologue after *The Sign of Jonas* (1953)

—in the hospital again, where there's
no odor of sanctity. Fumes of isopropyl,
not incense, fill the air of every room.
Still, nurses wear white gauze masks
and sterile walls distract the appetite.

Here in the world I reject the senses.
At ten, Dr. Roser begins to trim inches
of bone and membrane from the septum
inside my bulbous, Picasso nose. As he prunes
my *cupiditas*, blood blossoms everywhere.

A novice nurse turns green as snot and flees
the room, renouncing my flesh. Yet Sister Liz
holds fast, both fingers rosary beads and mops
my brow with a handkerchief, as if I'd carried
my own cross from Gethsemani's garden.

Next thing I know they trundle my bed
into the hall and a whiff of salvation wafts
over me; I lean on my left elbow like a guest
at Caesar's evening banquet, my pulped proboscis
aiming toward the cafeteria kitchen. Later,

I dream of feasting on pungent loaves and fishes.
When I wake to winter light, I retreat to an empty,
cloistered room, and on Father Osborne's Underwood
transform twenty unleavened sheets of paper
into the ending of *Bread in the Wilderness*.

After the Sack of South Carolina: W. Gilmore Simms in Exile

Columbia, March 1865

The night of fire, the negroes, terrified,
Skulked into their huts, lay low in darkness,
While Yankees wolfed down whiskey, bottle
After bottle, dumping what they could not drink
Onto the flames that flared from twenty windows
On the Isaacs' block alone. Columbia
Is blackened boards and ashes, hardly far
Enough from Woodlands, which we have deserted
To hide out during Sherman's march downstate.
The stragglers we've seen here ignited fears
We left behind.
                           Last week we learned our home,
Rebuilt from cinders just three years ago,
Had burned again—ten-thousand books consumed
Like papers wrapped round fat cigars. The Northern
Generals denied their part; I'm shamed to say
At first I blamed the man they pointed to, the man
Their war is meant to save. Yet neighbors say
That Nimmons carried out my writing desk
And chair and watched his step so both were spared.

So now I cannot sleep, remembering
How Woodlands burned the first time: bright light pouring
From the sundered roof, tongues licking in
The upper rooms and halls—seconds until
A thousand bricks and boards
Let go—when Nimmons ran a ladder up
And rescued me, who now has let him down.

Summer Storm

After dark, barbarian winds stormed around
The house and lightning lit up windows
Everywhere; rain ricocheted across
The roof, against the vinyl siding. We stayed
In bed until it passed, then fell asleep.
We never looked out back.
                              I saw
It first, in light softly redefining what
We think we know for sure — our tulip poplar,
Planted jointly when our love was new,
Had lost its top, the upper trunk and limbs
Lopped off and flung awkwardly over chairs
Akimbo on the deck.
                              Upstairs, you saw
Sky start to blush and heard the sweet birds sing,
Battening down their broken nests.

September 22, in Indiana

It's the first day of fall—already cold—
And the wind blows hard, blasting Arctic air
That should have died out over Michigan,
Caught in the eye teeth of Keewanaw's pines,
Or splintered into driftwood west of Windsor.

Here, swaying elms let loose of yellow leaves
That flash against the iron sky, like sunsets
Over water. Suddenly, I'm chilled but stay
On guard, reminded how, when evening fell
Last night, I heard a honk and looked up from

My book to geese cresting the nearby woods
And the surging darkness I did not see coming.

Before Taking Your Picture
I Think Of

the snapshot when you're twenty-three again.
Your eyes, like lapis, catch the light and stare
back, thrilled. I wonder which of many men
fingered the button this time, unaware

you smile at him still. It's been twenty years
since his hand's hair brushed your spongy breast
and felt the warmth that rises in your ears
when sweetly whispering censored words. Caressed

again by my late gaze, your lips comply
and part, as if they're willing but somehow
cannot let go the past. Do pictures lie?
If so, some later man might wish he were me now.

Granary Days

At dusk, when August haze would glow on corn
Like attic dust, we'd head for Edwardsville,
The Missouri sun behind us, blazing in
The liquid lap of the Mississippi. We'd
Have slaved since morning, painted clapboard dormers
From jerry-built platforms, or cut green lawns
In Ladue the size of outfields — all day
Waiting for night to come. And then, at last,
We went: rode by Cahokia Mounds, toward
The darkness, to the Granary Bar, its parking
Lot lights just turning on the moment we
Got there.
                           Much later, at last call,
We'd leave, our ears and hearts ringing, our eyes
Beer-bleary and red from gawking, lovesick
With girls we'd never get. Homeward, the air
Flew through us like a salve, drugged us, blocked out
What only now I recognize:
Mist creeping up in darkness like regret,
Possibilities I couldn't get my arms
Around, not till now, now that it's too late,
The Granary bare, its doors boarded shut.

First Kiss

We'd hidden from the nuns behind a wooded lot
and let our lips slip into place, lubricious
pulped tongues about to touch: I felt a rush

of pleasure piqued by sin. It felt as though
we'd stolen into our neighbor's cellar
and pried into his stash of cobwebbed boxes —

postcards in French, pin-up girls, parts of guns —
while upstairs lumbering above us, he made
the floorboards sway, like treetops about to fall.

At Mercouri's Restaurant

For Jake

               Mornings, mist rose
off the cold water when the sun poured in,
lighting a path to shore where anchored boats
bobbed and strained. Mercouri'd stand among
the empty outdoor tables, staring at the waves
and yearning for the world he'd left behind.

               One day at lunch
Hellas came to him: a boy not twelve
and Aphrodite, bronzed skin glimmering
against a top that gripped her torso tight.
She nibbled at some perch, sipped half a Tab,
then swiveled her long legs and tilted face

to meet his fish-eyed gaze head on—
but by the time he could advance she'd slipped
outside again into the blinding light.
He felt like swine that Circe had no itch for.
Among their plates he found a glass of water
overturned: under it, the coins she'd touched

shining in clear view, but out of reach.

A Divorcée's Revenge

Hearing your poisoned voice again today
Makes me think of the great Christian martyrs
Like Agatha who, when ripped from sackcloth
And sandals like leftovers from Glad Wrap,
Then raped, raped again, and finally rolled
Over forty feet of burning coals,
Never once lost her smile — not until blisters
Blurred what had been her lips. And I as well
Won't budge: you hate my "Goddamned guts" for what
I've got and won't give up — our kids, my neck.
But now I've cut the wires, to keep my cool,
And love all the wide world that is not you.

After Delivering My Son to the Ex

Almost thirteen hours and pounds of sweat
Later, I'm back in town, already full
Of missing him the next two months. Along
The road, sunflowers leaned like fishing poles,
Tilting toward the west, as if dark, strong

Currents were pulling the light down, down and out
Of reach. I hunger for my son who's got
Away. I stop at work to check the mail,
Wanting human contact, but find that
Man my wife has left me for; he fails

To see me, for his head's submerged into
The dumpster, like a well from which one drinks.
Quickly I open the door, then pause to quip,
"Looking for your lunch?" Just now it sinks
In: what he eats won't ever have to touch my lips.) x

The Fair Oaks Apartments Revisited

I've come to see again the place
We spent our year as newlyweds.
Two decades and divorce erase
What <u>drew us from our separate be</u>ds.

From a park bench across the street
The brick and windows seem the same
And the oaks out front complete
The picture giving it its name.

And yet the lives we lived inside
Belonged to other people, whom
I'd never recognize; I've tried
To bury that young bride and groom.

White gulls with black-tipped wings are wheeling
Overhead, criss-crossing west
To east and back; one pair is squealing
As if a crow couched in its nest.

Washington Avenue Bridge

Minneapolis, Good Friday, 2000

Fifteen years gone, and now I'm back, a ghost
Returned to a world no longer in my mind.
It's drained of color, like a faded shirt
That keeps its form but little else and fits
The stranger at Goodwill much better than
It ever suited me. The river curves
Left a hundred yards beyond the bridge,
A snake unspooling the slow, heavy waters
Of March. The dimpled surface scintillates,
But the wind's so cold no one's here, and air
Rings with caws of hawks huddled in trees
On the bare western banks. A hundred yards
More, the relentless river cuts right, bending
Under another bridge — and rolls out of sight.

Crossing this bridge each morning, I would look
Out the bus window: framed, for a moment,
The distant bridge — thick with cars — glittered in
The sun that overbrimmed the eastern bluffs.
The feeling stirring in my blood exceeded
All words — the way my spirit now can feel
No spot to ground itself. I've twice replaced
Every cell since moving to a town
Downriver. I have been away so long
I'm dead to this strange place, where my old life
Was lived by someone else. And yet the waters
Keep flowing, no two waves the same, the current
Carrying them onward and downward out of sight,
The same sun shining on their passage to the sea.

48

IV

Downtown at Dusk

Now that day is gone, a gray half-light
Is filling in the open spaces
Between buildings shut to the coming
Dark. Twilight erodes the bony
Branches of trees whose black hands
Hold up the gold of last leaves,

While the western moon, like a lamppost,
Patiently waits to light the night up.

Lake Petworth, Sunrise

After J.M.W. Turner

In the last minutes of dawn, deer come
To drink the cold waters, fog lapping round
Them like the darkness of old woods. They've waited
All night to slake their thirst. But when the sun
Cuts through the mist that softens the world's edge,

They vanish — lost like prayers we don't remember,
Blind to desire in the blunt light of day.

Epiphanies

For Beverley

The December we met I buried my past.
I drove to a funeral on New Year's Eve
And watched fog peel back like molting skin:
My windshield cleared to a dark farm
Where white birds were nursing the upturned ground,
While above, black ones flew into the distance.

Much later that night, I saw you downtown,
Framed by French doors that opened as you stepped
Outside, arms letting go. As if gazed at
Through gauze, your dress shimmered red as pressed flesh.
It was then the light changed: I turned and passed
A darkened church, its north curb clear of cars—

Though round the block I saw its single square
Of light, whose flare carries even now chords
Of an organ impressed by lonely, passionate hands.

Merton in Love

sonnet

personna poen

June 1966

Two months ago, bedridden at St. Joe's,
My body numbed, my wracked back fixed, I woke
And met M's eyes: Love-struck? Had I a choice?
I dove into the waters, where each stroke
Plunged me into the greater depths. What's real

double meaning

Is inmost. Since we "borrowed" Brother Jim's
Unlocked sedan, I've been reborn, can feel
In us the freedom of the woods that brims
Over every branch and naked root.
Though we'll get caught like sophomores, she'll linger
In the subsoil of my wild mind. I doubt
A lot, but not that each twig feels her fingers:
Love lives in solitude; M's touch has powers
The abbot can't ban—even in cold showers.

Preheating

Midsummer, heat lingers like flannel in the dusk,
beading Martini glasses with sweat. We touch
our drinks together, lightly, so they clink
like strangers at an airport grazing satchels.

We forget the gas grill heating on the porch,
the green beans simmering on the stove;
we only know desire, can only sense
the warmth that waits in the other's grasp.

Upstairs, like passengers, we don't look down
on what we left below, coals glowing in the dark
like distant cities; nor to what awaits us — missed
connections, ruined food. Instead, we fly

into a banquet of flesh, blackening our bodies
on the grills of each other's bones, fillets
cooked fast on highest heat, but eaten slow.

Weekend Retreat in Brown County

Sunday, in oblique October light, we drive
Toward town, toward famous Main Street's

Knickknack boutiques; we pass trees
Dripping from night's hard rain, their blonde

Leaves glinting like beaten gold, and wind
Along a curvy creek, edging abrupt bends

And loops—when gravel grips us in a bottlenecked
S: before us, two deer staring like statues through

The glare of tinted windows. And then they
Enter a crack in the wild woods. Quickly

We park and walk across Beanblossom Bridge.
It lifts us over the teeming creek and leaves

Us amid crowding brush and canopies of pines,
Nine yards from where the buck and doe had vanished.

But now we've lost our path: we either turn
Back toward town, or improvise a way

To cut through the new growth, which long ago
Closed us out of the woods' darkness.

double nen

Leaving San Francisco Early

. . . the dead . . . reach us most easily just as we awaken.
—Saul Bellow, Humboldt's Gift

At four a.m., Pacific Heights is still,
Though your wife's in bed and aches for love
Already, pillow packed between her legs.

Random street lamps cut through the dark and stir
The sleeping mind like a tall cup of Peet's,
Steaming its dawn fog. This is the hour

The North Beach tide starts to slacken and makes
The quiet waves opaque. It's now in dreams
The dead come back, the ghosts we won't let in

Our thoughts once we're awake, on guard. But now
You're mesmerized by window squares of light
Whose shimmering refuses to harden under

The layered sheets of mist. You feel like
A ghost yourself, merging into the space
Between tall buildings, passing through a landscape

Luminous and strange and soon to disappear
When the stark light of morning wakes your wife
And returns the world of pressing, solid things.

On the Beara Peninsula

I sit here sipping a Sonoma Merlot
in southwest Ireland, taking in the view:

The sun has set the coast on fire, cresting
a hill of broken rocks and fuchsia hedges,

and Coulagh Bay's a luminous blue.
Beyond, the Atlantic tends to black,

so soon the fields will steep in night,
will mark what's missing, what's lost beneath

the starless sky on land and sea.
                        Yet out my window
gnats are basking in a golden haze —

hanging in mid-air. So I do what can be done:
Hold up my cup to the light, while the light lasts.

Adagio for Middle Age While Sitting Outside in Late October

The open window lets
Me hear, though muffled through the shade, the strings
 Play Barber's themes of last regrets
  And irrecoverable things.

The evening light can't compensate.
It fades beyond the neighbor's fence, which showers
 The yard with darkness, like a crate
  Overturned on flowers.

So now I'll take indoors
My present potted life. Inside the house,   *double meaning*
 You walk across the hardwood floors
  Unbuttoning your blouse,

Where light—like that far past
The fence, but brighter—irradiates our room:
 Our candles burn down way too fast,
  But nip night's early bloom.

*rhyme - sometimes -
I wish he
wouldn't rhyme!*

V

persona poem?

Signs of Life

*It took 31 days for former Indiana Gov. Edgar Whitcomb to sail
the Atlantic and even after returning he's not sure why he made
the trip.*
— Terre Haute *Tribune Star*, 3/26/90 *great quote*

Sometimes I close my eyes and I'm still
At sea, catching the cold Atlantic trade winds
That rode the looping hills of gray-green waves
And whipped white spume in my face like aftershave.
My month between the Ghana coast and the Caribbean
I lived another lifetime, was someone else.
Each splash would spank me wider awake,
And made me think I'd slept through those four years
Back home in Indiana. There, landlocked, I'd breathed in,
Each day, dust from dry fields as I drove
Back roads to and from the capitol, my lungs
Nearly full, two vacuum bags choked with ashes.
Nothing I'd promised had come to pass; no one
Took a chance. I never did what I had to do.
Last year, I turned seventy-two, then pushed off

From a rickety dock moored to African earth
In a thirty-foot craft. I was the last man in waters wide
As Mars. At dusk, the sun went down, a fireball
Burning the line that stitched the sky
To sea like lit gasoline. It would glow
Above the horizon's rim long after moonlight
Fell, glimmering amid whitecaps and western waves.
When the sails drooped and the moon anchored
Overhead, I'd nap on my back, waiting
For wind and rain to crack the night. Once,
I woke to a vortex of white and black swirling
Round the boat, sucking it
Inward while waterfalls belted mast, tackle, and flapping

Canvas; I hugged the jib and held my breath, bricks
Of saltwater tumbling all over. Somehow,
Like Brendan in his boat of hides and timber,
I survived the weather's wish to turn me into
Jetsam. Dawn came, and once again flying fish
Gave signs of life and I was on the move
Cooking oatmeal and coffee, trimming
Sails, mopping deck, fidgeting with depth charts
Or sextants — always moving, always looking for wind
To shift, for sharks to surge, for land to meet
My blue unblinking eyes.
                              So now, back home
Again, I'm bored; things seem the same as ever.
And yet at night, if deep sleep comes, I dream
Lucid dreams, about sleek fish surfing
Through keyholes of reef, water currents streaming
Down their gills like air lifting the light wings
Of a Cessna whose pilot guides it beyond the clouds.

could see ending coming
but I still like it

Henry James Shaves at 57 (New Year's, 1900)

great title

Scarred from the cutting words that chafed and sliced
The face of his last new play, Henry James
Can't sense the past and dreads the new year's iced-
Over windows, marquées lacking names.

They turn him toward the shaving glass: Gray streaks
Disfigure who he used to be, like ashes
Transformed from burned up books. He scrapes his cheeks
As clean as shoveled steps, except for patches

Of raw, red skin. Not since the Civil War
Has Henry felt this light. A change like weather
Thaws out his heart and loosens the *cri de coeur*
"Live all you can" — the voice of Lambert Strether

In Gloriani's Paris garden, where
A younger James once chatted up Flaubert.

Regarding the Old Poets, after the Reading

For D.H. and W.D.S.

Donald Hall?
william Stafford?
W. D. Snodgrass

Lagging their hosts by fifty feet,
the great ones — bent by abundance,
laden like fruit trees in fall —
lug their bags of books, limping:

a pair of sapling pines has framed them
and fixes their forms where western light
ignites the path they pace along,
bathing them in brilliance —
                              I hold the glow
in mind, then turn away before
they shuffle into the parking lot
overripened with shadows.

Skylights

When my grandmother died, sky —
white as if embalmed — buried
roads and parking lots with snow.
The next day, though, as we drove
to her grave in north St. Louis
the sun penetrated ice like light
pulsing through glass tubes.

I remembered then a hot June night,
months before: late, I'd walked
by a huge house lit from rathskeller   cap
to rafters, Mozart thundering
through its open door, while above
stars splintered like bones withdrawing
into the cold folds of earth.

Winter Landscape

After C.D. Friedrich's oil, 1811

In old age life's become a winter landscape.
The traveler has come so far, through snow
Above his shins, through drifts between his knees.

Like hammered rocks, his bones crack when he slams
The crutches down, then like a pendulum
Swings the weight of an antique clock across

The miles and miles of frozen swells and flats.
This unmapped land's as uncompliant as
The god he'd begged to save his pregnant wife.

But that's all past. In Friedrich's winter scene
The snow has nearly stopped; he rests against
A rock by intermeshing firs, which guard

Him from the mortal storm. But note he's holding
Up his blistered palm as if it oozed
Like Christ's. It's clear he soon will die, but not

Forsaken: Friedrich's put a crucifix
Amid the trees—as if within the mind
Of this old man—and makes this place

A sacred spot, like the steeples rising out
Of sight, in mist unveiling what has always
Been there, that's everywhere he goes.

Watching the Sun Set from the Mount St. Francis Cemetery

Late afternoon, I walk the Stations of
The Cross—12 wooden silhouettes embedded
Beneath bare trees in a secluded gully.

When I step foot again on level ground,
A band of glowing orange stretches across
The distant treetops to the west, and above

A range of clouds—almost maroon—soon shades
To black. Beside the two new heaps of earth
And hay, I find a limestone bench and watch

The sky. Here, I remember the hopeless hunt
For my grandparents' stones ten years ago;
The unkempt grounds—grown wild—consumed what marked

Their loss. It felt like death had come again.
But now, I feel at peace and wait beside
The recent plantings till, as white as slabs

Not yet inscribed, the winter stars return.

Memorial Field, 1973

I'm standing on a hill, high
Behind the batter's box, where my brother
Digs in, alive, his full-count tip ⌐
Tumbled from the catcher's web. ⌐

The stars are out, and in deep left
A new moon's rising, like the grapefruit
Change a guy named Grace threw me here
Three years ago. My father

Missed that game, the June that cancer
Ruled his skies. But now he's telling
Me how good he feels, his nights
Shining once again, like insects

Swarming in the August glow
Below us, which will not dim until
The game is over, my brother ⌐
 Stunned by a roundhouse curve. ⌐

Turning Point
in the European Theater

New Year's Day, 1945, my father marched
With Patton's Army to the Western Front,
The weather cold as a meat-locker, raw
And threatening sleet. Next day, they watched as snow
Fell and fell and the Moselle River turned *spelling?*
To ice, while generals, far off, planned to push

Them across the Siegfried Line and into hills
Dark with Nazi snipers—and from there
To victory. Here Dad would later pose
By walls unraveling, their threads loose and frayed.
Behind him in the river, "Hitler's Bridge,"
One side already sunk in frigid waters.

But weeks before in France, Dad thought he'd freeze
While sleeping. Patton came to kick their butts
And boost the troops' morale: "My men can eat
Their belts," he growled. And: "Anyone who loots
I'll shoot." Yet, Dad had sneaked into a vacant
House, quickly grabbed two woolen quilts, then stepped

Outside—at once he'd pressed both shoulder blades
Against the doorless jamb and held his breath:
Not two arm-lengths away appeared a jeep
In back of which sat Patton, just then turning
His head when the jeep jerked right to avoid
Some ice, like a marksman, startled by flares,

Who lifts a hand off the gun to shade his eyes.

Illuminations

New Year's, my father got the word—
"Five months to live." Then cardinals
Came to our snow-glazed ash,
A blaze amid the bloodless drifts.
The next night we woke to thunder
Above the roof, and our room luminous
As a flood light under water.

Now May has bloomed Dad's backyard green
And the world from his old bay window
Brims with new light. It's now I realize
High in the oak above the house
A mourning dove has come, its singular coos
Consoling the empty sunlit rooms.

Reprise

A Saturday in June, the lawn is mown
and the late afternoon light makes the glass
of the storm door shine; only it is between

me and a flash of memory: Brubeck playing,
my father's front door open; just-cut grass
glowing in the glare of forty years ago,

and him, like me, abruptly glad to be
alive, right now, as a new breeze blows through
the maple's greenest leaves and "Take Five" fills

the house, a lung in rhythm with the notes.

The Gargoyle in Our Backyard

> *. . . only two patients are alive and free of tumor at the time of*
> *this report, both 7 years after resection. . . .*
> —"Oat Cell Carcinoma of the Lung: A Review of
> 138 Cases." *Cancer* 23.3 (1969).

Forty years ago, my father made medical history:
Staved off the cancer storming in his lung,
A squall that had sunk everyone else on board
His boat, capsized in cold, uncharted waters.
Last year, dismantled off our coast, he foundered
For good. We planted what's left in our inland grove.⌐

All day, today, the western sky wore black,
Widowed young by a sun buried too soon.
At five, the darkness drove east, then unleashed
The grief of straight-line winds that leveled
Our ancient elm as if it had no roots.
It crashed across the fence whose white boards

Flattened like broken teeth. But amid the split spar
And a thousand chips, the gargoyle stands intact:
It guards the bits of bone and ash shipwrecked
Beneath it, emboldened by what survives.

About the Poet

Matthew Brennan was born in St. Louis and educated at St. Louis University High. He earned a B.A. from Grinnell College and Master's and Doctoral degrees from the University of Minnesota. He is the author of two previous collections of poems, *Seeing in the Dark* (1993) and *The Music of Exile* (1994), as well as the verse-narrative *The Sea-Crossing of Saint Brendan* (2008). His poems have appeared widely in such publications as *Poetry Ireland Review*, *Notre Dame Review*, *South Dakota Review*, *Poet Lore*, *Sewanee Review*, and *Blue Unicorn*. He has also written two critical studies — *Wordsworth, Turner, and Romantic Landscape* (1987) and *The Gothic Psyche* (1997) — and has contributed articles and reviews to *South Carolina Review*, *South Atlantic Quarterly*, *Sewanee Review*, *Georgia Review*, *The Wordsworth Circle*, *English Language Notes*, and other journals. In 1999 he won the Thomas Merton Prize for Poetry of the Sacred. He lives in Terre Haute with his wife, Beverley Simms, and teaches at Indiana State University.

LaVergne, TN USA
06 November 2009
163309LV00004B/1/P